Searching for Light

Written by Alanna Zabel

Illustrated by Rita Vigovszky

Published by AZIAM Books.
© 2004 by Alanna Zabel.
All rights reserved.

ISBN-13: 978-0-9884449-4-2

AZIAM Books
Santa Monica, CA
www.aziam.com

AZ AM
BOOKS

Between two islands in the Pacific Ocean
Swam a beautiful mermaid named Luz.
Being half fairy and half human
She understood diverse and different worlds.

On one island lived the Wise Men,
Choosing spiritual paths and lives.
Warriors lived on the other island
They hunted to survive.

Luz was floating on the ocean's surface,
Basking in the glorious sun rays.
Pokey Pelican swam near, whispering,
"I challenge you to a test today."

"What kind of test? Luz asked.
"Math, Science, or Verse?"
"None of the above," Pokey answered.
"To win, you'd be the first."

Luz was immediately intrigued,
Swimming close to Pokey's face.
"Tell me! I will do it!"
"I will win this race!"

"Winning is difficult," Pokey said.
"Because it is you against you."
"I don't care how hard it is," Luz answered
"Just tell me what to do!"

"Very well," snapped Pokey
"I will skip all of my warnings."
"Your fierce independence"
"Just might be your curse and your glory."

"Down on the ocean's floor,"
"Lies a very powerful gem."
"It has the ability to solve the riddle"
"Of Earth's great problem."

"It is the bridge that links humanity"
"To their spiritual truth."
"Once discovered, all beings will be equal,"
"Thanks to you."

"You're beating around the bush," Luz said.
"I may be young, but I'm not dumb!"
"You are talking in riddles,"
"Just tell me what to do, and it will be done!"

"That's it, snooty Luzy,"
Pokey chuckled in her face.
"You're on your own, big girl,"
"Off to your own big race."

Pokey spread his wings to fly away.
Luz' face turned pale white.
"What do you mean 'that's it'?" she asked.
As Pokey flew out of sight.

"What's the big deal?" Luz thought,
"Swim to the ocean floor and back,"
"Pick up a jewel while I am down there,"
"Curing Earthlings from their lack."

"I'll be a heroine, a Queen!"
"Savior to all,"
"Leading the blind to light,"
"And deterring Earth's great fall."

Balancing above the ocean,
Luz was excited by her new quest.
She looked from shore to shore,
As the Wise Men gathered for her test.

"Your time has come, young Luz,"
Said the Wise Men tribe.
Sounds of jestery and mockery
Came from the other side.

The Wise Men sat in a circle,
Closing their eyes to meditate.
"We'll support you in silence," they said,
"You must unravel your own fate."

A woman from the Warrior Island yelled,
"I baked some fresh homemade bread today."
Luz turned and swam to get some,
Putting her quest on delay.

Men from Warrior Island
Started laughing out loud.
"She's already given up!" they yelled,
"There's our Savior. Aren't we proud?!"

Their menacing words ended her hunger,
She thought, "I will show them!"
"They'll be singing my praises"
"When I solve Earth's problem!"

With great force from her tail,
She plunged towards the ocean floor,
"I am a Goddess on a mission,"
"A distracted mortal, no more!"

The pressure of the ocean's depth
Began squeezing her tight.
She was holding her breath
With all of her might.

Overwhelmed with fear,
Luz turned herself around.
With a strong kick of her tail,
She was surface bound.

Humiliated again,
Luz turned her pain into strength.
Diving again under water,
Intending to swim the full length.

Determined and focused,
Motivated by spite.
She swam so far towards the bottom,
Until she no longer saw light.

Luz couldn't see anything
Without light to reflect.
She lost all sense of direction,
Scrambling for any object.

Her hand touched something moving.
Which yanked her body sharp.
Holding on very tightly...
To what was the fin of a shark!

The shark whipped her about,
Forcing out all of her breath.
Desperately needing fresh air,
She thought she'd surely meet death.

Instead, the shark swam to the surface,
Throwing Luz towards a large rock.
Pummeled by the crashing waves,
She clung there in shock.

Feeling scared and alone,
She was cold and bleeding.
She didn't know where to move
To escape each wave's beating.

Taking a leap of faith,
Luz jumped into the water once more.
Too tired to swim, though,
She was washed back to shore.

Laying on the sand
Bleeding and broken,
Luz felt like a failure
As her humility was woken.

"What was I trying to do?"
She asked, "Put on a show?"
"Do I want to help Earth?"
"Or inflate my ego?"

"A real Savior offers kind service,"
"Not needing admiration or fame."
"A silent, loving, and pure presence,"
"Is what would make a great change."

Too tired to move,
Too exhausted to speak,
Luz closed her eyes.
She fell deep asleep.

The tide began to rise,
The water rushed in to shore.
Cleansing Luz' wounds,
While shifting the sand floor.

Luz remained deep asleep
As she drifted to sea.
No resistance, no fighting,
No more "Me, Me, Me."

She dreamt of the Wise Men
Supporting her somehow,
Sending her beams of light,
Keeping their vow.

"Don't listen to the mockery," they said,
"They're just jealous of you."
"We applaud your noble efforts,"
"Joy shines through all that you do."

Luz' body began to sink
Although she remained asleep.
She could breathe underwater,
As she floated down deep.

As Luz sank to the bottom,
She settled on the ocean floor.
Her body shifted the sea dust,
Revealing a door.

The door handle was a diamond
The size of a tire.
The door was a mirror
Surrounded in sapphire.

When Luz hit the cold mirror,
She immediately woke up again.
One glance at the door,
And she leaped for the GEM!

She pulled on the diamond,
Not realizing that it was a door.
Her reflection appeared aggressive,
And she was saddened once more.

Luz's reflection spoke to her, saying,
"Accept everything as it is - nothing else,"
"Then you become a mirror"
"For others to see their true self."

"I know that your intentions are pure,"
"That you care deeply for all beings."
"Learn to witness your emotions, and"
"Match your actions with your feelings."

As Luz let go of the diamond,
The door opened quickly to the right.
A strong current pulled her inside,
Where she could see a distant light."

A beautiful rainbow appeared.
Embracing Luz' body tight.
Each color was glorious by itself,
But together they created radiant light.

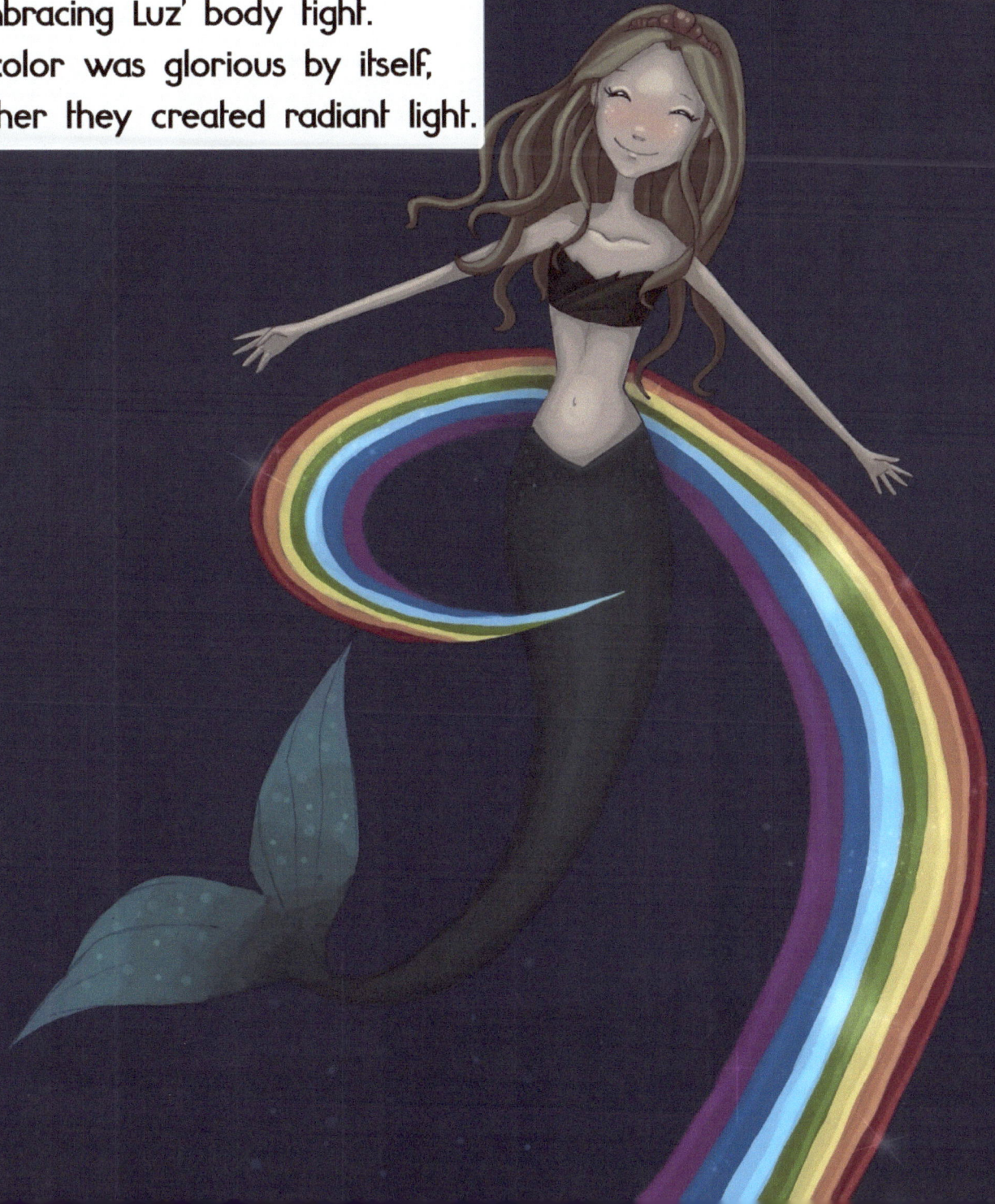

The light carried Luz to the surface,
Where it extended out wide.
One side on the Warrior Island,
And one on the Wise Men's side.

Pokey flew down,
Sitting on the rainbow's edge.
"You did it! I am impressed,"
"Congratulations," he said.

"But I have no jewel. I failed,"
Luz said, sinking her head low.
"By surrendering, you won," Pokey said,
"It's about the journey, not the goal."

"I owe you so much gratitude," Luz said,
"Yet I was selfish and mean."
"Parents are often left thankless," Pokey said,
"I'm in great company."

They watched the Rainbow Bridge
Connecting the two worlds as one.
Can you imagine the Earth being
Separated from the Sun?

Division destroys,
Unison creates.
Let's all work together to make
Our world a peaceful place.

www.ingramcontent.com/pod-product-compliance
Lightning Source LLC
LaVergne TN
LVHW072112070426
835509LV00003B/126